Baby Blackhat Resistor Color Bands

By: Honey Beez

ISBN: 9798592670107
Back cover photo author: Adim kassn

DEDICATION

To my King Blackhat, children and family, and hacker children worldwide!

BABY BLACKHAT RESISTOR COLOR BANDS

What's a "resistor"?

A resistor is an electronic component that reduces electrical current that is flowing through a circuit. It lessens the voltage or electricity flowing through a circuit.

What is a "color band"?

A color band is a line of color or stripe that is located on a resistor electronic component. These stripes have different meanings. There can be 3 stripes, 4 stripes or 5 stripes on a resistor. We are only talking about 3 band resistors in this book. The first 2 stripes are the digits for the resistor amount. The third stripe is the multiplier.

Why do I need to memorize the color bands?

Memorizing the color bands is useful so that you know right away how strong a resistor is at lowering the electrical flow by looking at the resistor color bands quickly.

Resistors are measured in Ohms. With this symbol: "Ω"

Let's look at a chart of these color bands:

Photo author: Adim kassn

See the colors? We are going to memorize the color order with a story…

RESISTOR COLOR BAND STORY

Our color band story starts with a man named: **BBROY**

Photo author: Benjamin Shahn

BBROY's car was hard to tell the color. ☐

Some called BBROY's car BLACK.
Some called BBROY's car BROWN.

These are the first two color bands.
Black then Brown.

BBROY's name is the order of the first five color bands.
BLACK, BROWN, RED, ORANGE, then YELLOW.

These are the first five color bands.

BBROY didn't have enough GREEN, meaning money.
So he GOT BLUE, meaning sad.

These are the next two color bands, **GREEN** and then **BLUE**.

BBROY was sad over his girlfriend **VIOLET**.

Photo author: Tonata20

This is the next color band, <mark>VIOLET</mark>.

So he bought his girlfriend a GREY house with a WHITE picket fence.

These are the final two color bands. GREY and WHITE.

Photo author: Dsdugan

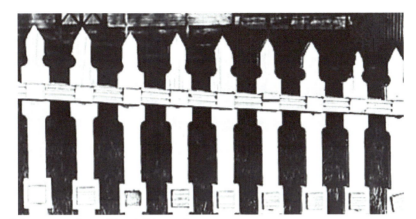

Photo author: Paul Strand

Let's hear that all again!

B	Black
B	Brown
R	Red
O	Orange
Y	Yellow
G	Green
B	Blue
V	Violet
G	Grey
W	White

BBROY's car that some called Black, some called Brown, didn't have enough Green and got Blue! He got blue over his girlfriend Violet! So he bought her a Grey house with a White picket fence.

1ˢᵗ DIGIT	2ⁿᵈ DIGIT	3ʳᵈ DIGIT
0	0	0
1	1	1
2	2	2
3	3	3
4	4	4
5	5	5
6	6	6
7	7	7
9	9	9

Now Let's Practice!

What is the resistor color band for the following resistors?

প্রথম ব্যান্ড
দ্বিতীয় ব্যান্ড
গুণক
টলারেন্স

Photo author: Sumita Roy Dutta

(Just the first three color bands)

RED
VIOLET
GREEN

Write out your colors with the corresponding digits 0-9 and the multiplier:

B	0	0	10^0 (1)
B	1	1	10^1
R	2	2	10^2

O	3	3	10^3
Y	4	4	10^4
G	5	5	10^5
B	6	6	10^6
V	7	7	10^7
G	8	8	10^8
W	9	9	10^9

RED	first digit is 2
VIOLET	second digit is 7
GREEN	multiplier is 10^8

Use a calculator and multiply 27 by 10 to the power of 8!
You get:

2.7 Mega ohms or 2.7MΩ

Photo author: Jon Sullivan

More Practice:

What is the resistor amount of this resistor?

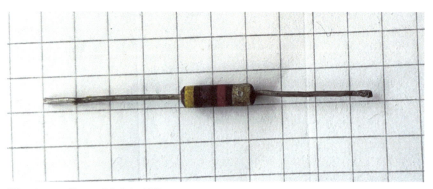

Photo author: YoktoBit

YELLOW
VIOLET

RED

Write out your colors with the corresponding digits 0-9 and the multiplier:

B	0	0	10^0 (1)
B	1	1	10^1
R	2	2	10^2
O	3	3	10^3
Y	4	4	10^4
G	5	5	10^5
B	6	6	10^6
V	7	7	10^7
G	8	8	10^8
W	9	9	10^9

Use a calculator and multiply 47 by 10 to the power of 2!
You get:

4.7 K ohms or 4.7KΩ

Another! What would the resistance bee
for this resistor?

Photo author: Användare:Chrizz

Careful now, this picture shows the
resistor backward. You can tell because
the first stripe shown is Gold, a
tolerance band, that we aren't talking
about here. So Start your calculation
from the other side of the resistor!

RED
BLACK
YELLOW

Write out your colors with the corresponding digits 0-9 and the multiplier:

B	0	0	10^0 (1)
B	1	1	10^1
R	2	2	10^2
O	3	3	10^3
Y	4	4	10^4
G	5	5	10^5
B	6	6	10^6
V	7	7	10^7
G	8	8	10^8
W	9	9	10^9

Use a calculator and multiply 20 by 10 to the power of 4!
You get:

200 K ohms or 200KΩ

Circuits:

What would the resistor colors be for the Resistor in this circuit? The Resistor is noted by the squiggly line and the "R":

Use a calculator to divide and look at our chart for the digits and multiplier:

B	0	0	10^0 (1)
B	1	1	10^1
R	2	2	10^2
O	3	3	10^3

Y	4	4	10^4
G	5	5	10^5
B	6	6	10^6
V	7	7	10^7
G	8	8	10^8
W	9	9	10^9

The first digit was 2, the second digit was 6 and it was multiplied by 10 to the power of 4:

RED
BLUE
YELLOW

ABOUT THE AUTHOR

Honey is a retired computer hacker
and mother.   Honey is an American
and a New Yorker. She has several
degrees, one in Industrial
Electronic Engineering for
computers and electronics.

www.ingramcontent.com/pod-product-compliance
Lightning Source LLC
LaVergne TN
LVHW072053060326
832903LV00054B/420